Philosophy of Logic

HARPER ESSAYS IN PHILOSOPHY

Edited by Arthur C. Danto

Arthur C. Danto	WHAT PHILOSOPHY IS
Norwood Russell Hanson	EXPLANATION AND OBSERVATION : A GUIDE TO PHILOSOPHY OF SCIENCE
Jerrold J. Katz	UNDERLYING REALITY OF LANGUAGE AND ITS PHILOSOPHICAL IMPORT
Norman Malcolm	PROBLEMS OF MIND
David Pears	WHAT IS KNOWLEDGE?
Hilary Putnam	PHILOSOPHY OF LOGIC
B. A. O. Williams	ETHICS
Robert Paul Wolff	IN DEFENSE OF ANARCHISM
Richard Wollheim	ART AND ITS OBJECTS

Philosophy of Logic

Hilary Putnam

A TORCHBOOK LIBRARY EDITION
Harper & Row, Publishers
New York, Evanston, San Francisco, London

PHILOSOPHY OF LOGIC. Copyright © 1971 by Hilary Putnam.

All rights reserved. Printed in the United States of America. No part of this book may be used or reproduced in any manner whatsoever without written permission, except in the case of brief quotations embodied in critical articles and reviews. For information address Harper & Row, Publishers, Inc., 49 East 33rd Street, New York, N.Y. 10016. Published simultaneously in Canada by Fitzhenry & Whiteside Limited, Toronto.

First TORCHBOOK LIBRARY EDITION published 1971.

STANDARD BOOK NUMBER (cloth): 06-136042-2

LIBRARY OF CONGRESS CATALOG CARD NUMBER: 71-149364

Contents

Preface

————◆•◆————

Many different philosophical issues arise in connection with logic. Some of these issues shade over into philosophy of mathematics (which will not be sharply distinguished from philosophy of logic in the present essay), while others shade over into philosophy of language and into the theory of knowledge. In the present essay I shall concern myself with the so-called ontological problem in the philosophy of logic and mathematics—that is, the issue of whether the abstract entities spoken of in logic and mathematics really exist. I shall also ask whether in logic itself (as distinguished from mathematics generally) reference to abstract entities is really indispensable, and I also shall take a look at the extent to which reference to such entities is necessary in physical science.

My aim in this essay will be not to present a survey of opinions on these problems, but to expound and defend one position in detail. Even if the reader is not convinced by my argument, it is hoped that he will find the present discussion valuable, if only in shaking up preconceptions and stimulating further discussion.

Philosophy of Logic

I.

What Logic Is

———————◆•◆•◆———————

Let us start by asking what logic *is,* and then try to see why there should be a philosophical problem about logic. We might try to find out what logic is by examining various definitions of "logic", but this would be a bad idea. The various extant definitions of "logic" manage to combine circularity with inexactness in one way or another. Instead let us look at logic itself.

If we look at logic itself, we first notice that logic, like every other science, undergoes changes—sometimes rapid changes. In different centuries logicians have had very different ideas concerning the scope of their subject, the methods proper to it, etc. Today the scope of logic is defined much more broadly than it ever was in the past, so that logic as some logicians conceive it, comes to include all of pure mathematics. Also, the methods used in logical research today are almost exclusively mathematical ones. However, certain aspects of logic seem to undergo little change. Logical results, once established, seem to remain forever accepted as correct—that is, logic changes not in the sense that we accept incompatible logical principles in different centuries, but in the sense that the style and notation that we employ in setting out logical principles varies enormously, and in the sense that the province marked out for logic tends to get larger and larger.

It seems wise, then, to begin by looking at a few of those principles that logicians have accepted virtually from the beginning. One such principle is the validity of the following inference:

(1)   All *S* are *M*
                All M are P
     (therefore) All *S* are *P*

Another is the Law of Identity:

(2)   *x* is identical with *x*.

Yet another is the *inconsistency* of the following:

(3)   *p* and not-*p*.

And still another principle is the validity of this:

(4)   *p* or not-*p*.

Let us now look at these principles one by one. Inference (1) is traditionally stated to be valid for all *terms S, M, P*. But what is a *term?* Texts of contemporary logic usually say that (1) is valid no matter what *classes* may be assigned to the letters *S, M,* and *P* as their extensions. Inference (1) then becomes just a way of saying that if a class S is a subclass of a class M, and M is in turn a subclass of a class P, then S is a subclass of P. In short, (1) on its modern interpretation just expresses the transitivity of the relation "subclass of". This is a far cry from what traditional logicians thought they were doing when they talked about Laws of Thought and "terms". Here we have one of the confusing things about the science of logic: that even where a prin-ciple may seem to have undergone no change in the course of the centuries—e.g., we still write:

> All S are M
> *All M are P*
> (therefore) All S are P

—the *interpretation* of the "unchanging" truth has, in fact, changed considerably. What is worse, there is still some controversy about what the "correct" interpretation is.

Principle (2) is another example of a principle whose correct interpretation is in dispute. The inter-pretation favored by most logicians (including the present writer) is that (2) asserts that the relation of identity is reflexive: everything bears this rela-tion (currently symbolized "=") to itself. Some philosophers are very unhappy, however, at the very idea that "=" is a relation. "How can we make sense of a *relation*," they ask, "except as something a thing can bear to *another* thing?" Since nothing can bear identity to a *different* thing, they conclude that whatever "=" may stand for, it does not stand for a relation.

Finally, (3) and (4) raise the problem: what does *p* stand for? Some philosophers urge that in (4), for example, *p* stands for any *sentence* you like, whereas other philosophers, including the present writer, find something ridiculous in the theory that logic is about *sentences*.

Still, all this disagreement about fine points should not be allowed to obscure the existence of a substantial body of agreement among all logicians—even logicians in different centuries. All logicians agree, for example, that from the premises

> All men are mortal
> All mortals are unsatisfied

one may validly infer

> All men are unsatisfied

even if they sometimes disagree about the proper *statement* of the general principle underlying this inference. Similarly, all logicians agree that if there is such a thing as the Eiffel Tower, then

> The Eiffel Tower is identical with the Eiffel Tower

and all logicians agree that (if there is such a thing as "the earth")

> The earth is round or the earth is not round

even if they disagree about the statement of the relevant principle in these cases too. So there *is* a body of "permanent doctrine" in logic; but it just doesn't carry one very far, at least when it comes to getting an exact and universally acceptable statement of the general principles.

II.

The Nominalism-Realism Issue

———————◆•■•◆———————

At this stage it is already clear that there are philosophical problems connected with logic, and at least one reason for this is also clear: namely, the difficulty of getting any universally acceptable statement of the general principles that all logicians somehow seem to recognize. If we explore this difficulty, further philosophical problems connected with logic will become clearer.

Philosophers and logicians who regard classes, numbers, and similar "mathematical entities" as somehow make-believe are usually referred to as "nominalists". A nominalist is not likely to say:

(A)   "For all *classes S, M, P:* if all *S* are *M* and all *M* are *P*, then all *S* are *P*".

He is more likely to write:

(B)   "The following turns into a true *sentence* no matter what *words* or *phrases* of the appropriate *kind* one may substitute for the letters *S, M, P:* 'if all *S* are *M* and all *M* are *P*, then all *S* are *P'*.''

The reason is clear if not cogent: the nominalist does not really believe that classes exist; so he avoids formulation (A). In contrast to classes, ''sentences'' and ''words'' seem relatively ''concrete'', so he employs formulation (B).

It is thus apparent that part of the disagreement over the ''correct'' formulation of the most general logical principles is simply a reflection of philosophical disagreement over the existence or nonexistence of ''mathematical entities'' such as classes.

Independently of the merits of this or that position on the ''nominalism-realism'' issue, it is clear, however, that (B) cannot really be preferable to (A). For what can be meant by a ''word or phrase of the appropriate kind'' in (B)? Even if we waive the problem of just what constitutes the ''appropriate kind'' of word or phrase, we must face the fact that what is meant is all *possible* words and phrases of some kind or other, and that *possible words and phrases* are no more ''concrete'' than classes are.

This issue is sometimes dodged in various ways. One way is to say that the appropriate ''phrases'' that one may substitute for *S, M, P* are all the ''one-place predicates'' in a certain ''formalized language.'' A formalized language is given by completely specifying a grammar together with the meanings of the basic expressions. Which expressions in such a language are one-place predicates (i.e., class-names, although a nominalist wouldn't be caught dead calling them that) is specified by a formal grammatical rule. In fact, given a formalized language L, the class of permissible substitutions for the dummy letters S, M, P in

(5)   If all S are M and all M are P, then all S are P

can be defined with great precision, so that the task of telling whether a certain string of letters is or is not a "substitution-instance" of (1) (as the result of a permissible substitution is called) can even be performed purely mechanically, say, by a computing machine.

This comes close to satisfying nominalistic scruples, for then it seems that to assert the validity of (5) is not to talk about "classes" at all, but merely to say that all substitution-instances of (5) (in some definite L) are true; i.e., that all the *strings of letters* that conform to a certain formal criterion (being a substitution-instance of (5) in the formalized language L) are true. And surely "strings of letters" are perfectly concrete—or are they?

Unfortunately for the nominalist, difficulties come thick and fast. By a logical *schema* is meant an expression like (5) which is built up out of "dummy letters", such as S, M, P, and the logical words if-then, all, some, or, not, identical, is (are), etc. Such schemata have been used by logicians, from Aristotle to the present day, for the purpose of setting out logical principles (although Aristotle

confined his attention to a very restricted class of
schemata, while modern logicians investigate all possible schemata of the kind just described). A schema
may be, like (5), a "valid" schema—that is, it
may express a "correct" logical principle (what
correctness or validity is, we still have to see), or it
may be "invalid". For example,

If some S are P, then all S are P

is an example of an invalid schema—one that fails
to express a correct logical principle. Ancient and
medieval logicians already classified a great many
schemata as valid or invalid.

Now, defining valid is obviously going to pose
deep philosophical issues. But the definition of
valid we attributed to the nominalist a moment
ago, viz., a schema S is valid just in case all substitution-instances of S *in some particular formalized
language L* are true—is unsatisfactory on the face
of it. For surely when I say that (5) is valid, I mean
that it is correct *no matter what class-names* may be
substituted for S, M, P. If some formalized language
L contained names for all the classes of things that
could be formed, then this might come to the same as
saying "all substitution-instances of (5) in L are
true". But it is a theorem of set theory that *no* language L *can* contain names for *all* the collections of
things that could be formed, at least not if the
number of things is infinite.

To put it another way, what we get, if we adopt

the nominalist's suggestion, is not *one* notion of
validity, but an infinite series of such notions:
validity in L_1, validity in L_2, validity in L_3, . . .
where each notion amounts simply to "truth of all
substitution-instances" in the appropriate L_i.

We might try to avoid this by saying that a schema
S is valid just in case all of its substitution-instances
in every L are true; but then we need the notion of
all possible formalized languages—a notion which
is, if anything, *less* "concrete" than the notion of a
"class".

Secondly, the proposed nominalistic definition of
validity requires the notion of "truth." But this is a
problematic notion for a nominalist. Normally we do
not think of material objects—e.g., strings of actually
inscribed letters (construed as little mounds of ink
on paper) as "true or "false"; it is rather *what the
strings of letters express* that is true or false. But the
meaning of a string of letters, or what the string of
letters "expresses", is just the sort of entity the
nominalist wants to get rid of.

Thirdly, when we speak of *all* substitution-instances of (5), even in one particular language L,
we mean all *possible* substitution-instances—not just
the ones that happen to "exist" in the nominalistic
sense (as little mounds of ink on paper). To merely
say that *those instances of (5) which happen to be
written down are true* would not be to say that (5)
is valid; for it might be that there is a false substitution-instance of (5) which just does not happen

to have been written down. But *possible* substitution-instances of (5)—*possible* strings of letters—are not really physical objects any more than classes are.

One problem seems to be solved by the foregoing reflections. There is no reason in stating logical principles to be more puristic, or more compulsive about avoiding reference to "nonphysical entities", than in scientific discourse generally. Reference to classes of things, and not just to things, is a commonplace and useful mode of speech. If the nominalist wishes us to give it up, he must provide us with an alternative mode of speech which works just as well, not just in pure logic, but also in such empirical sciences as physics (which is full of references to such "non-physical" entities as state-vectors, Hamiltonians, Hilbert space, etc.). If he ever succeeds, this will affect how we formulate all scientific principles—not just logical ones. But in the meantime, there is no reason not to stick with such formulations as (A), in view of the serious problems with such formulations as (B). [And, as we have just seen, (B), in addition to being inadequate, is not even really nominalistic.]

To put it another way, the fact that (A) is "objectionable" on nominalistic grounds is not really a difficulty with the science of logic, but a difficulty with the philosophy of nominalism. It is not up to logic, any more than any other science, to conform its mode of speech to the philosophic demands of nominalism; it is rather up to the nominalist to provide a satisfactory reinterpretation of such assertions as (5), and of any other statements that logicians (and physicists, biologists, and just plain men on the street) actually make.

Even if we reject nominalism as a demand that we here and now strip our scientific language of all reference to "nonphysical entities", we are not committed to rejecting nominalism as a philosophy, however. Those who believe that in truth there is nothing answering to such notions as class, number, possible string of letters, or that what does answer to such notions is some highly derived way of talking about ordinary material objects, are free to go on arguing for their view, and our unwillingness to conform our ordinary scientific language to their demands is in no way an unwillingness to discuss the philosophical issues raised by their view. And this we shall now proceed to do.

We may begin by considering the various difficulties we just raised with formulation (B), and by seeing what rejoinder the nominalist can make to these various difficulties.

First, one or two general comments. Nelson Goodman, who is the best-known nominalist philosopher, has never adopted the definition of validity as "truth of all substitution-instances". (It comes from Hugues Leblanc and Richard Martin.) However, Goodman has never tackled the problem of defining logical validity at all, so I have taken the liberty of discussing the one quasi-nominalistic attempt I have seen. Secondly, Goodman denies that nominalism is a restriction to "physical" entities. However, while the view that only physical entities (or "mental particulars'', in an idealistic version of nominalism; or mental particulars and physical things in a dualistic system) alone are real may not be what Goodman intends to defend, it is the view that most people understand by ''nominalism'', and there seems little motive for being a nominalist apart from some such view. (The distinction between a restriction to ''physical entities'' and a restriction to ''mental particulars'' or ''physical things and mental particulars'' will not be discussed here, since it does not seriously affect the philosophy of logic.)

The first argument we employed against formulation (B) was that this formulation, in effect, replaces our intuitive notion of validity by as many notions of validity as there are possible formalized languages. Some logicians have tried to meet this difficulty by the following kind of move: Let L_0 be a formalized language rich enough to talk about the positive integers, and to express the notions ''x is the sum of y and z'' and ''x is the product of y and z''. Let L_i be any other formalized language. Let S be a schema which has the property that all its substitution-instances in L_0 are true (call this property the property of being ''valid-in-L_0'', and, analogously, let us call a schema ''valid-in-L_i'' if all its substitution-instances in L_i are true). Then it is true—and the proof can be formalized in any language rich enough to contain both the notions of ''truth in L_0'' and ''truth in L_i''—that S also has the property that all its substitution-instances in L_i are true. In other words, *if a schema is valid-in-L_0, it is also valid-in-*

L_i. So, these logicians suggest, let us simply define
"validity" to mean *valid-in-L_0*. If S is valid, it
will then follow—not by definition, but by virtue of
the meta-mathematical theorem just mentioned—
that all of its substitution-instances in L_i are true, no
matter what language L_i may be. So "validity" will
justify asserting *arbitrary* substitution-instances of
a schema (as it should, on the intuitive notion).

To this, one is tempted to reply that what I *mean*
when I say *"S* is valid" *directly* implies that *every*
substitution-instance of S (in *every* formalized language) is true. On the proposed definition of valid
all that I *mean* when I say that *"S* is valid" is that
S's substitution-instances *in L_0* are true; it is only a
mathematical fact, and not part of what I mean that
then S's substitution-instances in *any* language are
true. Thus the proposed definition of valid completely fails to capture the intuitive notion even if it
is coextensive with the intuitive notion.

This reply, however, is not necessarily devastating. For the nominalistic logician may simply reply
that he is not *concerned* to capture the "intuitive"
notion; it is enough if he can provide us with a notion
that is philosophically acceptable (to him) and that
will do the appropriate work.

Be this as it may, the fact remains that the language L_0 is one that itself requires talking about
"mathematical entities" (namely *numbers*), and
that the proof of the statement that "if S is valid-in-
L_0, then S is valid-in-L_i" requires talking about
arbitrary expressions of L_i (i.e., about all *possible*

expressions of L_i). Thus neither the language L_0 nor the meta-mathematical theorem just mentioned is really available to a *strict* nominalist, i.e., to one who foreswears *all* talk about "mathematical entities".

The second argument we used was that the notion of "truth" is not available to a nominalist. However, this claim is extremely debatable.

Our argument was, in a nutshell, that "true" makes no sense when applied to a physical object, even if that physical object be an inscription of a sentence; it is not the physical sentence that is true or false, but *what the sentence says*. And the *things* sentences say, unlike the sentences (inscriptions) themselves, are not physical objects.

The natural response for a nominalist to make here would, I think, be to distinguish between

(6) S is true

and

(7) S is true as understood by Oscar at time t.

If S is a physical object (say, a sentence-inscription), then (6) makes little sense indeed, save as an elliptical formulation of some such fact as (7). But (7) represents a perfectly possible relation which may or may not obtain between a given inscription, an organism, and a time. (How reference to "times" is to be handled by the nominalist, I shall not inquire; perhaps he must identify a "time" with a suitable three-dimensional cross section of the whole four-dimensional space-time universe.) Why should it not be open to the nominalist to assert that some *sentences* are *true* in the sense of having the relation occurring in (7) to suitable organisms at suitable times? Granted that that relation is a complex one; the burden of proof is on the realist to show that that relation essentially presupposes the existence of nonphysical entities such as propositions, meanings, or what have you.

Another form of the second argument takes the form of an "appeal to ordinary language". Thus, it is contended that

(8)   John made a true statement

is perfectly correct "ordinary language" in certain easily imagined situations. Now there are two possibilities: (a) that (8) implies that statements exist (as nonphysical entities); or (b) that (8) does not imply this. In case (b) there is no problem; we may as well go on talking about "statements" (and, for that matter, about "classes", "numbers", etc.), since it is agreed that such talk does not imply that statements (or numbers, or classes) exist as non-physical entities. Then nominalism is futile, since the linguistic forms it wants to get rid of are philosophically harmless. In case (a), since (8) is true and (8) implies the existence of nonphysical entities, it follows that these nonphysical entities do exist! So nominalism is false! Thus nominalism must be either futile or false.

Against this the nominalist replies that what he wishes to do is to find a "translation function" that will enable us to replace such sentences as (8) by sentences which do not even *appear* to imply the existence of nonphysical entities. The effect of this will, he thinks, be to provide us with a terminology which is conceptually less confusing and more revealing of the nature of reality than the terminology we customarily employ. To be sure, such sentences as (8) are "philosophically harmless" if correctly understood; but the problem is to make clear what this correct understanding is.

The nominalist can strengthen this somewhat by adding that it is not necessary, on his view, that the translation function preserve *synonymy*. It is enough that the proposal to understand such sentences as (8) on the model of their nominalistic translations should be a good one, in the sense of conducing to increased clarity.

Thus the fact that in "ordinary language" the words "true" and "false" are normally applied to "statements" does not convince the nominalist *either* that statements really exist as nonphysical entities, *or* that a departure from ordinary language [in, say, the direction of (7)] is an intellectual sin.

Finally, there is the "argument" that what (7) *means* is: there is a *statement* which S "expresses" to Oscar at time *t*, and that *statement* is true. According to this argument, (7) involves a disguised reference to a nonphysical entity (what S "expresses"), and is thus not "really" nominalistic.

This argument reduces either to the appeal to ordinary language just discussed or else to the mere claim that *really* only *statements* (construed as nonphysical entities expressed by sentences) can be "true" or "false". Since this claim is precisely what is at issue, this is not an argument at all, but a mere begging of the question.

All arguments that notion of truth is unavailable to the nominalist seem thus to be bad arguments. On the other hand, it does not follow that the nominalist is simply *entitled* to the notion. Truth [or the triadic relation between inscriptions, organisms, and times that occurs in (7)] is hardly a primitive thing like "yellow", so surely the nominalist owes us *some* account of what it is; an account consistently framed within the categories of his metaphysics. If he cannot provide such an account (and what nominalist has?), his right to use the notion does become suspect.

Before the reader (or the nominalist) replies too hastily with *tu quoque,* let him be reminded of the following facts: the "intuitive" notion of truth seems to be inconsistent (cf. the well-known logical antinomies in connection with it); but given any formalized language L, there is a predicate "true-in-L" which one can employ for all scientific purposes in place of the intuitive true (when the statements under discussion are couched in L), and *this* predicate admits of a *precise* definition using only the vocabulary of L itself plus set theory.[1] This is not

1. This was shown by Tarski. For a semipopular exposition see "The Semantic Conception of Truth" in *Readings in Philosophical Analysis,* ed. H. Feigl and W. Sellars (New York, 1949), pp. 52–84.

wholly satisfactory—one would prefer a single predicate true to an infinite collection of predicates "true-in-L_1", "true-in-L_2", etc.—but it is not unbearable, and the antinomies give strong reason to doubt that any notion of truth applicable to *all* languages and satisfying the intuitive requirements could be consistent. The realist is thus in a position not to explain the intuitive notion of truth, but to provide a battery of alternative notions that he can use in all scientific contexts as one would wish to use true, and that he can precisely define. But—today, at least—the nominalist cannot even do this much.

Our third argument was that reference to *all* the sentences of a formalized language (or even all the substitution-instances of a fixed schema) is not reference to "inscriptions" (since it can hardly be supposed that all the infinitely many sentences of any formalized language are actually inscribed somewhere) but to abstract entities—"possible inscriptions", or, according to some authors, to the "types" or shape-properties which inscriptions exemplify. (These types are supposed to "exist" independently of whether any inscriptions actually exemplify them or not; thus, they too are nonphysical entities.) When we say "all substitution-instances of (S) are true", we mean *even those substitution-instances that no one has actually written down*. Thus these "substitution-instances"—especially the "potential" ones—are no more "physical" than classes are. To my knowledge, no rejoinder to this argument worth considering exists.

Our reconsideration of the three arguments has, thus, not altered our conclusion that (B) is not a nominalistic formulation. We see, however, that the deeper one goes into the first two of the three arguments the more complex (and also the more technical) the arguments are going to become.

We may summarize the upshot of this section by saying that at present reference to "classes", or something equally "nonphysical" is indispensable to the science of logic. The notion of logical "validity", on which the whole science rests, cannot be satisfactorily explained in purely nominalistic terms, at least today.

III.
The Nominalism-Realism Issue
and Logic

The issue of nominalism vs. realism is an old one, and it is interesting to review the way in which it has become connected with the philosophy of logic. Elementary logic has enunciated such principles as (2), (4), (5), has listed such patterns of valid inference as (1), and has asserted the inconsistency of such forms as (3) since Aristotle's day. Modern "quantification theory", as the corresponding branch of modern logic is called, or "first-order logic with identity", has an ·immensely larger scope than the logic of Aristotle, but the topic of concern is recognizably similar.

The basic symbols are:

(i)   "Px" for "x is P", and similarly, "Pxy" for "x bears P to y", "$Pxyz$" for "x, y, z stand in the relation P", etc.

(ii)   "(x)" (read: "for every x") to indicate that every entity x satisfies a condition; i.e., "$(x)Px$" means "every entity x is P".

(iii)   "(Ex)" (read: "there is an x such that")
to indicate that some (at least one) entity
x satisfies a condition; i.e., "$(Ex)Px$"
means "there is an entity x which is P".

(iv)   "$=$" (read: "is identical with") for identity, i.e.; "$x = y$" means "x is identical with
(is one and the same entity as) y".

(v)   "$\cdot$" for "and", "v" for "or", "$-$" for
"not", e.g., "$(Px \text{ v } -Qx) \cdot Rx$" means
"either x is P or x is not Q; and x is R".

In addition the symbols $\supset$ (read: "if . . . then")
and $\equiv$ (read: "if and only if") are used with the
definitions: "$Px \supset Qx$" ("If Px then Qx") is short
for "$-(Px \cdot -Qx)$", and "$Px \equiv Qx$" is short for
"$(Px \supset Qx) \cdot (Qx \supset Px)$".

In this notation we can write down all the principles that Aristotle stated. E.g., (5) becomes:

(5′) $((x)(Sx \supset Mx) \cdot (x)(Mx \supset Px)) \supset (x)$
$(Sx \supset Px)$.

Also, by considering the full class of schemata that
we can write with this notation, we are led to consider potential logical principles that Aristotle never
considered because of his general practice of looking
at inferences each of whose premises involved exactly *two* class-names.

The most important thing, however, is that with
modern notation we can analyze inferences which
essentially involve two-or-more-term *relations;* it

was essentially the failure to develop a logic of relations that trivialized the logic studied before the end of the nineteenth century, and that makes that logic—the traditional logic from Aristotle on, and even including the work of Boole, tremendously important as it was for later developments—utterly inadequate for the analysis of deductive reasoning in its more complicated forms.

In his many logical and philosophical writings, Quine has urged that quantification theory does not really assert, for example, formulation (A) of the preceding section. On Quine's view, when a logician builds a system one of whose theorems is, say, (5′), he does not thereby mean to assert (A). Rather, in (5) or (5′), *S, M, P* are mere "dummy letters" standing for *any predicate you like;* and what the logician is telling you is that *all substitution-instances* of (5) or (5′) are truths of logic.

On this view, the following is a "truth of logic":

(9)   If all crows are black and all black things absorb light, then all crows absorb light.

But the general principle (A):

For all classes *S, M, P:* if all *S* are *M* and all *M* are *P*, then all *S* are *P*

is not a truth of *logic,* on Quine's view, but a truth of *mathematics.*

Now, then, I do not much care just where one draws the line between logic and mathematics, but this particular proposal of Quine's seems to me hardly tenable.

My reasons are principally two. In the first place, logical tradition goes against Quine; for, from the beginning it has been the concern of logicians to state just such general principles as (A) and *not* to "sort out" such truths as (9) from other truths. In the second place, I don't think all substitution-instances of a valid schema *are* "true": some are obviously meaningless. For example:

(10)   If all boojums are snarks and all snarks are eggelumphs, then all boojums are egge-lumphs

does not appear to me to be a true statement—it has the *form* of a logically valid statement, but, I think, it is not a statement at all, and neither true nor false. Indeed, to call (10) true requires some revision of the usual logical rules. For it is a theorem of standard logic that if a statement of the form "if p and q, then r" is true, then either p and q are both true and r is true, or p is true and q false and r true (or false), or p is false and q true and r true (or false), or p and q are both false and r is true (or false). But in the case of (10) the three components corresponding to $p, q,$ and r are *neither* true *nor* false.

Of course, one could adopt the decision to extend the notion of truth and to call any statement that has the form of a logically valid statement true. But then

(11)   All boojums snark or not all boojums snark

(which has the form p v $-p$) would have to be counted as true, and this seems extremely misleading, since normally anyone who asserts (11) would be understood to be committed to:

(12)   The statement that all boojums snark is either true or false.

In my view, logic, as such, does *not* tell us that (9) is true: to know that (9) is true I have to use my knowledge of the logical principle (A), *plus* my knowledge of the fact that the predicates *"x* is a crow", *"x* is black" and *"x* absorbs light" are each true of just the things in a certain class, namely the class of crows, (respectively) the class of black things, (respectively) the class of things which absorb light. Even this "knowledge" involves a certain idealization: namely, ignoring the fact that some of these predicates (especially black) are ill-defined (neither true nor false) in certain cases. However, even if we are willing to make this idealization, knowing that, say, *"x* is a crow" is a predicate which is true (apart from possible borderline cases) of each thing in a certain class and false of each thing in the complement of that class is knowing a good bit about both language and the world. That *"x* is a crow" is a pretty well-defined predicate, *"x* is beautiful" is pretty ill-defined, and *"x* is a snark" is meaningless, is not *logical* knowledge, whatever kind of knowledge it may be.

We have thus a disagreement between Quine and me, since it is just such statements as (9) that Quine regards as "truths of logic", while according to me each such statement reflects a complicated mixture of logical and extralogical knowledge. But it is not important that the reader should agree with me here and not with Quine—all I insist on, for present purposes, is that the decision to call such statements as (A) "principles of logic" is not ill-motivated, either historically or conceptually. There may be some choice here, to be sure; but it is important that one quite natural choice makes statements like (A), which refer explicitly to classes, part of *logic*.

The logical schemata so far considered have contained (x) [*for every individual x*] and (Ex) [*there exists an individual x such that*], *but not* (F) and (EF). Thus, given a "universe of discourse" we can say, with the notation as so far described, that some element of the universe is P by writing (Ex) Px, but we cannot say that there is a *set* or *class* of all the elements with the property P (in symbols: (EF) (x) $(Fx \equiv Px)$), because we don't have "(EF)".

The decision of the great founders of modern logic—Frege, and, following him, Bertrand Russell—was unhesitatingly to count such expressions as (EF) as part of logic, and even to allow expressions such as (EF^2), with the meaning *for every class of classes*, (EF^3) with the meaning *for every class of classes of classes*, etc., as part of "logic".

My contention here is that there was no mistake in

so doing. Their decision may not have been the only possible decision—indeed, in the introduction to the second edition of *Principia Mathematica,* Russell carefully refrains from claiming that it was—but it represented a perfectly natural choice. The question of where to "draw the line" (if we want to draw a line at all) between logic and set theory (and hence between logic and mathematics) is one which has no nonarbitrary answer.

Suppose, however, we decide to draw the line at "first-order" logic ("quantification theory") and to count such expressions as (EF), (EF^2), etc., as belonging to "mathematics". Still, we are left with the problem: when a logician builds a system which contains such theorems as (5′), *what does he mean to be asserting?* He may, of course, not mean to be asserting anything; he may just be constructing an uninterpreted formal system, but then he is certainly not doing logic. The simple fact is that the great majority of logicians would understand the intention to be this: the theorems of the system are intended to be valid formulas. Implicitly, if not explicitly, the logician is concerned to make assertions of the form "such-and-such is *valid*"; that is, assertions of the kind (A). Thus even first-order logic would normally be understood as a "metatheory"; insofar as he is making assertions at all in writing down such schemata as (5′), the logician is making assertions of validity, and that means he is implicitly making second-order assertions: for to assert the validity of the first-order schema (5′) is just to assert

$(S)(M)(P)$ (schema 5′)—and this is a second-order assertion.

In sum, I believe that (a) it is rather arbitrary to say that "second-order" logic is not "logic"; and (b) even if we do say this, the natural understanding of first-order logic is that in writing down first-order schemata we are implicitly asserting their validity, that is, making second-order assertions. In view of this, it is easy to see why and how the traditional nominalism-realism problem came to intensely concern philosophers of logic: for, if we are right, the natural understanding of logic is such that all logic, even quantification theory, involves reference to classes, that is, to just the sort of entity that the nominalist wishes to banish.

IV.
Logic vs. Mathematics

———◆•••◆———

In view of the foregoing reflections, it is extremely difficult to draw a nonarbitrary line between logic and mathematics. Some feel that this line should be identified with the line between first-order logic and second-order logic; but, as we have just seen, this has the awkward consequence that the notions of validity and implication[2] turn out to belong to mathematics and not to logic. Frege, and also Russell and Whitehead, counted not only second-order logic but even higher-order logic (sets of sets of sets of . . . sets of individuals) as logic; this decision amounts to saying that there is no line "between" mathematics and logic; mathematics is part of logic. If one wishes an "in-between" view, perhaps we should take the one between second- and third-order logic to be the "line" in question. However, we shall not trouble ourselves much with this

---

2. A is said to *imply* B, just in case the conditional $(A \supset B)$ with A as antecedent and B as consequent is *valid*. In short, "implication is validity of the conditional".

matter. The philosophical questions we are discussing in this essay affect the philosophy of mathematics as much as the philosophy of logic; and, indeed, we shall not trouble to distinguish the two subjects.

V.

The Inadequacy of Nominalistic Language

———◆•◆•◆———

By a "nominalistic language" is meant a formalized language whose variables range over individual things, in some suitable sense, and whose predicate letters stand for adjectives and verbs applied to individual things (such as "hard", "bigger than," "part of"). These adjectives and verbs need not correspond to observable properties and relations; e.g., the predicate "is an electron" is perfectly admissible, but they must not presuppose the existence ~~of such~~ of such entities as classes or numbers.

It has been repeatedly pointed out that such a language is inadequate for the purposes of science; that to accept such a language as the only language we are philosophically entitled to employ would, for example, require us to give up virtually all of mathematics. In truth, the restrictions of nominalism are as devastating for empirical science as they are for formal science; it is not just "mathematics" but physics as well that we would have to give up.

To see this, just consider the best-known example
of a physical law: Newton's law of gravitation.
(That this law is not strictly true is irrelevant to the
present discussion; the far more complicated law
that is actually true undoubtedly requires even more
mathematics for its formulation.) Newton's law, as
everyone knows, asserts that there is a force f_{ab} ex-
erted by any body a on any other body b. The direction of the force f_{ab} is towards a, and its magnitude
F is given by:

$$F = \frac{gM_aM_b}{d^2}$$

where g is a universal constant, M_a is the mass of a,
M_b is the mass of b, and d is the distance which sepa-
rates a and b.

I shall assume here a "realistic" philosophy of
physics; that is, I shall assume that one of our important purposes in doing physics is to try to state
"true or very nearly true" (the phrase is Newton's)
laws, and not merely to build bridges or predict experiences. I shall also pretend the law given above
is correct, even though we know today that it is only
an approximation to a much more complicated law.
Both of these assumptions should be acceptable to a
nominalist. Nominalists must at heart be material-
ists, or so it seems to me: otherwise their scruples are
unintelligible. And no materialist should boggle at
the idea that matter obeys some objective laws, and
that a purpose of science is to try to state them. And
assuming that Newton's law is strictly true is some-

thing we do only to have a definite example of a physical law before us—one which has a mathematical structure (which is why it cannot be expressed in nominalistic language), and one which is intelligible to most people, as many more complicated physical laws unfortunately are not.

Now then, the point of the example is that Newton's law has a content which, although in one sense is perfectly clear (it says that gravitational "pull" is directly proportional to the masses and obeys an inverse-square law), quite transcends what can be expressed in nominalistic language. Even if the world were simpler than it is, so that gravitation were the only force, and Newton's law held exactly, still it would be impossible to "do" physics in nominalistic language.

But how can we be sure that this is so? Even if no nominalist has yet proposed a way to "translate" such statements as Newton's law into nominalistic language, how can we be sure that no way exists?

Well, let us consider what is involved, and let us consider not only the law of gravitation itself, but also the obvious presuppositions of the law. The law presupposes, in the first place, the existence of forces, distances, and masses—not, perhaps, as real entities but as things that can somehow be measured by real numbers. We require, if we are to use the law, a language rich enough to state not just the law itself, but facts of the form "the force f_{ab} is $r_1 \pm r_2$", "the mass M_a is $r_1 \pm r_2$", "the distance d is $r_1 \pm r_2$", where r_1, r_2 are arbitrary rationals. (It is not necessary, or indeed possible, to have a name for each real number, but we need to be able to express arbitrarily good rational estimates of physical magnitudes.)

But no nominalist has ever proposed a device whereby one might translate arbitrary statements of the form "the distance d is $r_1 \pm r_2$" into a nominalistic language. Moreover, unless we are willing to postulate the existence of an actual infinity of physical objects, no such "translation scheme" can exist, by the following simple argument: If there are only finitely many individuals, then there are only finitely many pairwise nonequivalent statements in the formalized nominalistic language. In other words, there are finitely many statements $S_1, S_2, \ldots, S_n$ such that for an arbitrary statement S, either $S \equiv S_1$ or $S \equiv S_2$ or $\ldots$ or $S \equiv S_n$, and moreover (for the appropriate i) $S \equiv S_i$ follows logically from the statement "the number of individuals is N".[3] But if we have

3. Here is a sketch of the proof of this assertion: suppose for example, $N = 2$ and introduce (temporarily) symbols "a" and "b" for the two individuals assumed to exist. Rewrite each sentence $(x)Px$ as a conjunction $Pa \cdot Pb$ and each sentence $(\exists x)Px$ as a disjunction $Pa \vee Pb$. Thus every sentence S of the language is transformed into a sentence S' without quantifiers. There are only finitely many atomic sentences (assuming the number of primitive predicates in the language is finite). If the number of these atomic sentences is n, then the number of truth-functions of them that can be written is 2^{2^n}. One can easily construct 2^{2^n} quantifier-free sentences which correspond to these 2^{2^n} truth-functions; then *any* sentence built up out of the given n atomic sentences by means of truth-functional connectives will be logically equivalent to one of these sentences $T_1, T_2, \ldots, T_{2^{2^n}}$. Moreover, if $S' \equiv T_i$ is a theorem of propositional calculus, then it is easily seen that $S \equiv (\exists a, b)(a \neq b \cdot T_i)$ is true in every two-element universe, and hence "the number of individuals is two" (this may be symbolized $(\exists a, b)(a \neq b \cdot (x)(x = a \vee x = b)))$ implies $S \equiv (\exists a, b)(a \neq b \cdot T_i)$. Thus, if we let $S_1 = ``(\exists a, b)(a \neq b \cdot T_1)"$, $S_2 = ``(\exists a, b)(a \neq b \cdot T_2)"$, $\ldots$, then (1) if the number of individuals

names for two different individuals in our "language
of physics", say, a and b, and we can express the
statements "the distance from a to b is one meter $\pm$
one centimeter", "the distance from a to b is two
meters $\pm$ one centimeter", etc., then it is clear that
we must have an *infinite* series of pairwise nonequivalent statements. (Nor does the nonequivalence
vanish given the premise "the number of individuals
is N"; it does not follow logically from that premise
that any two of the above statements have the same
truth value.) Thus any "translation" of "the language of physics" into "nominalistic language"
must disrupt logical relations: for any N, there will
be two different integers n, m such that the false
"theorem":

> If the number of individuals is N, then the distance
> from a to b is n meters $\pm$ one cm. $\equiv$ the distance from
> a to b is m meters $\pm$ one cm.

will turn into a true theorem of logic if we accept
the translation scheme. Thus a nominalistic language
is *in principle* inadequate for physics.

The inadequacy becomes even clearer if we look at
the matter less formalistically. The concept "distance in meters" is an extremely complex one. What
is involved in supposing that such a physical magni-

---

is *two*, then every sentence S is equivalent in truth-value to one of
the sentences $S_1, S_2, \ldots, S_{2^{2^n}}$; and (2) the sentence $S \equiv S_i$ (for the
appropriate i) is itself *implied by* the statement that the number of
individuals is two. The same idea works for any finite number of
individuals.

tude as distance can somehow be coordinated with *real numbers?*

One account (which I believe to be correct) is the following. It is clear that physics commits us to recognizing the existence of such entities as "spatial points" (or space-time points in relativistic physics), although the nature of these entities is far from clear. Physicists frequently say that space-time points are simply "events", although this is obviously false. Carnap and Quine prefer to think of points as triples of real numbers (or quadruples of real numbers, in the case of space-time points); however, this seems highly unnatural, since the identity of a spatial point does not intuitively depend on any particular coordinate system. I prefer to think of them as properties of certain events (or of particles, if one has point-particles in one's physics); however, let us for the moment just take them as primitive entities, not further identified than by the name "point". On any view, there is a relation $C(x, y, z, w)$ which we may call the relation of congruence, which is a physically significant relation among points, and which is expressed in word language by saying that the interval $\overline{xy}$ is *congruent* to the interval $\overline{zw}$. (I say "on any view", because there is a serious disagreement between those philosophers who think that this relation can be operationally defined and those who, like myself, hold that all so-called operational definitions are seriously inaccurate, and that the relation must be taken as primitive in physical theory.) Let us take two points (say, the end points of the standard meter in Paris at a particular instant) and call them a_1 and a_2. We shall take the distance from a_1 to a_2 to be *one*, by definition. Then we may define "distance" as a numerical measure defined for any two points x, y, as follows:

"The distance from x to y is r" is defined to mean that $f(x, y) = r$, where f is any function satisfying the following five conditions:

(1) $f(w, v)$ is defined (and has a nonnegative real value) on all points w, v.

(2) $f(w, v) = 0$ if and only if w is the same point as v.

(3) $f(w, v) = f(w', v')$ if and only if $C(w, v, w', v')$ holds (i.e., if and only if the interval $\overline{wv}$ is congruent to the interval $\overline{w'v'}$).

(4)   If w, v, u are colinear points and v is between w and u, then $f(w, u) = f(w, v) + f(v, u)$. (Here "colinear" and "between" can either be defined in terms of the C-relation in known ways, or taken as further primitives from physical geometry.)

(5) $f(a_1, a_2) = 1$.

It can be shown that there is a unique function f satisfying conditions (1)–(5).[4] Thus the content of

4. Strictly speaking, this is only true if we require that f be a *continuous* function from space-points to reals. However, this property of continuity can be expressed without assuming that we already have a metric available on the space-points. I have left this out in the text only to simplify the discussion.

the definition given above may also be expressed by saying that distance is defined to be the value of the unique function satisfying (1)–(5).

Let us call the account, above, a description of the "numericalization"[5] of the physical magnitude distance. The point of interest in the present context is this: that even if we take "points" as individuals, and the relation "$C\ (x, y, z, w)$" as primitive, still we cannot account for the numericalization of distance without quantifying over functions. (Of course, we might avoid the whole problem, by identifying points with triples of real numbers and using the Pythagorean theorem to provide a definition of distance; but then the relation "object O is at point P" would either have to be analyzed, or we would have to leave numericalization an essentially mysterious and unexplained thing.)

In short, even the statement-form "the distance from a to b is $r_1 \pm r_2$", where r_1 and r_2 are variables over rational numbers, cannot be explained without using the notion of a function from points to real numbers, or at least to rational numbers. For any constant r_1, r_2 an equivalent statement can be constructed quantifying only over "points"; but to explain the meaning of the predicate as a predicate of

5. The term used in every text on the philosophy of science is not "numericalization" but "measurement". I have coined this barbarous term in order to stress that the problem is *not* one of *measuring* anything, but of *defining* something—viz., a correspondence between pairs of points and numbers. The term "measurement" is a hangover from the days of operationalism, when it was supposed that measurement was prior to definition, rather than vice versa.

variable r_1, r_2, one needs some such notion as function or set. And the natural way, as we have just seen, even involves functions from points to reals.

It is easy for one and the same person to express nominalistic convictions in one context, and, in a different context, to speak of distance as something defined (and having a numerical value) in the case of àbritrary points x, y. Yet, as we have just seen, this is inconsistent. If the numericalization of physical magnitudes is to make sense, we must accept such notions as function and real number; and these are just the notions the nominalist rejects. Yet if nothing really answers to them, then what at all does the law of gravitation assert? For that law makes no sense at all unless we can explain variables ranging over arbitrary distances (and also forces and masses, of course).

VI.

Predicative vs. Impredicative Conceptions of "Set"

———◆◆◆———

The set $\{x, y\}$ with just the two elements x, y is called the unordered pair of x and y. In terms of unordered pairs one can define ordered pairs in various ways. Perhaps the most natural, though not the customary, way is this: pick two objects a and b to serve as "markers". Then identify the ordered pair of x and y with the set $\{\{x, a\}, \{y, b\}\}$—i.e., with the unordered pair whose elements are the unordered pair $\{x, a\}$ and the unordered pair $\{y, b\}$. Let us adopt the notation $<x, y>$ for this ordered pair, i.e., $<x, y>$ is defined to be $\{\{x, a\}, \{y, b\}\}$. Then it is easily seen that for any x, y, u, v:

$$<x, y> = <u, v>$$

if and only if $x = u$ and $y = v$. Thus, two "ordered pairs" are identical just in case their elements are the same and are also ordered the same—which is all that is required of any definition of ordered pair.

In mathematics, a two-place relation is simply a

set of ordered pairs. Since "ordered pair" has just been defined in terms of "unordered pair", and "unordered pairs" are simply sets, it follows that "relation" can be defined in terms of the one primitive notion *set*. If R is a relation such that for all u, v, y

$$\text{if } <u, v> \varepsilon R \text{ and } <u, y> \varepsilon R, \text{ then } v = y$$

then the relation R is called a "function". Since function has just been defined in terms of relation (and the notion "$=$" which we count as part of elementary logic), it follows that function has been defined in terms of *set*.

It is well known that the natural numbers 0, 1, 2, 3, . . . can be defined in terms of *set*, in various ways. For example, one can identify 0 with the empty set, 1 with {0}, then 2 with {0, 1}, then 3 with {0, 1, 2}, etc. Also, the elementary operations "plus", "time", etc., can all be defined from the notion of *set*. Rational numbers are naturally identified with ordered pairs of natural numbers with no common divisor (and such that the second member of the ordered pair is not zero); and real numbers may be identified with series of rational numbers, for example, where a "series" is just a function whose domain is the natural numbers. Thus all of the "objects" of pure mathematics may be built up starting with the one notion *set;* indeed, this is the preferred style in contemporary mathematics.

Instead of saying, therefore, that physics essentially requires reference to functions and real numbers, as we did in the previous section, we could simply have said that physics requires some such notion as *set*, for the notions of number and function can be built up in terms of that notion. In the present section we shall make a cursory examination of the notion of a set.

The most famous difficulty with the notion of a set is this: suppose we assume

(1)   Sets are entities in their own right (i.e., things we can quantify[6] over).

(2)   If ϕ is any well-defined condition, then there is a set of all the entities which satisfy the condition ϕ.

Then (assuming also that the condition "$\sim x \ \varepsilon \ x$" is well defined), it follows that there is a set of all those sets x such that x does not belong to x. If y is that set, then

$$(3) \qquad (x) \ (x \ \varepsilon \ y \equiv \ \sim x \ \varepsilon \ x).$$

But then, putting y for x,

$$(4) \qquad y \ \varepsilon \ y \equiv \ \sim y \ \varepsilon \ y$$

—and this is a self-contradiction!

Obviously, then, one of our assumptions was false. Which could it have been? We could say that "$\sim x \ \varepsilon \ x$" is not a well-defined condition. But if $x \ \varepsilon \ y$ is a well-defined relation, for arbitrary sets x, y, then it would seem that $x \ \varepsilon \ x$, and also $\sim x \ \varepsilon \ x$, would have to

6. To "quantify over" sets means to employ such expressions as "for every set x" and "there is a set x such that".

be well-defined (in the sense of having a definite truth value) on all sets x. To give up either the idea that $x \, \varepsilon \, y$ is a well-defined relation or the idea that sets are entities we can quantify over would be to give up set theory altogether. But the only alternative is then to give up (or at least restrict) (2), which is highly counterintuitive.

One way out of the difficulty is the so-called theory of types. On this theory, "$x \, \varepsilon \, y$" is well defined only if x and y are of the appropriate types, where individuals count as the zero type, sets of individuals as type one, sets of sets of individuals as type two, etc. On this theory, "$\sim x \, \varepsilon \, x$" is not even grammatical since no set can be said either to be or not to be a member of itself. One can ask whether a set belongs to any set of the next higher type, but not whether it belongs to itself (or to any set which is not of the next higher type).

Let R be some relation among individuals. A set α such that for all x, if $x \, \varepsilon \, \alpha$, then $y \, \varepsilon \, \alpha$, for at least one y such that Rxy, will for the moment be called an *R-chain*. Suppose we want to say that there is some *R*-chain containing an individual U. Then we write:

(5) $\qquad (\exists \alpha)(\alpha \text{ is an } R\text{-chain}. \, U \, \varepsilon \, \alpha)$

where "α is an R-chain" is short for "$(x) \, (x \, \varepsilon \, \alpha \supset (\exists y)(y \, \varepsilon \, \alpha \cdot Rxy))$".

Now, the set β of all such U—all U such that some R-chain contains U—is a perfectly good set according to the theory of types, and also according to most mathematicians. Some few mathematicians and philosophers object to the idea of such a set, however. They argue that to define a set β as the set of all U such that there is an R-chain containing U is "vicious" because the "totality in terms of which β is defined"—the totality of all R-chains α—could contain β itself. In general, these mathematicians and philosophers say that a set should never be defined in terms of a "totality" unless that totality is incapable of containing that set, or any set defined in terms of that set. This is, of course, rather vague. But the intention underlying all this is rather interesting.

Suppose I do not understand the notion of a "set" at all, and, indeed, suppose I employ only some nominalistic language N. Suppose, now, that one day I decide that I understand two notions which are not nominalistic, or, at any rate, whose nominalistic status is debatable: the notions of "formula" and "truth". In terms of these notions I can introduce a very weak notion of set. Namely, suppose I identify sets with the formulas of my nominalistic language which have just one free variable x—e.g., the set of red things I identify with the formula 'Red(x)'. The notion of "membership" I explain as follows: if y is an individual and α is a "set" (i.e., a formula with one free variable 'x'), then "$y \; \varepsilon \; \alpha$" is to mean that α is true of y, where a formula $\phi(x)$ is true of an individual y just in case the formula is true when x is interpreted as a name of y. Thus, if α is the formula "Red(x)", we have

　　$y \, \varepsilon \, \alpha$ if and only if α is true of y

　　i.e., if and only if "Red(x)" is true of y

　　i.e., if and only if y is red.

So "Red(x)" turns out to be the "set of all red things"—as it should be.

I call this a "weak" notion of set, because it still makes no sense to speak of *all* sets of individuals, let alone sets of higher type than one—one can speak of all formulas, to be sure, but that is only to speak of all sets of individuals definable in N. If new primitives are added to N, then, in general, the totality of sets in the sense just explained, will be enlarged. However, one can iterate the above procedure. That is, let N' be the language one obtains from N by allowing quantification over all sets of individuals definable in N, N'' the language we obtain from N' by allowing quantification over all sets of individuals definable in N', etc. Then all of these sets of individuals—the ones definable in N, in N', in N'', . . . are examples of "predicative" sets: each of these sets presupposes a "totality" which is defined "earlier" (starting with the totality of individuals) and which does not presuppose it. (One can also introduce predicative sets of higher type, in terms of formulas about formulas, but this will not be done here.) The point that concerns us now is this: this notion of set, the predicative notion of set, is one which can be explained, up to any given level in the series N, N', N'', . . . in terms of quantifying only over sets definable earlier in the series, and this whole way of speaking

—of "sets definable in N", "sets definable in N' ", etc.—can itself be regarded, if one wishes, as a mere *façon de parler,* explainable in terms of the notions of formula and truth.

In contrast to the foregoing, if one ever speaks of all sets of individuals as a well-defined totality, and not just all sets definable in some one language in the series $N, N', N'', \ldots$, then one is said to have an impredicative notion of set.

VII.

How Much Set Theory
Is Really Indispensable for Science?

———————◆•◆•◆———————

In the foregoing, we argued that the notion set (or some equivalent notion, e.g., function) was indispensable to science. But we must now ask: does science need the "strong" (impredicative) notion of set, or only the "weak" (predicative) notion? For if we are interested in the nominalism-realism issue at all, we must not assume that the only alternatives are (a) nominalism, and (b) acceptance of the full notion "all sets" (or even, "all sets of individuals."). If we are inclined to be nominalistic at all, we may wish to keep our non-nominalistic commitments as weak as possible; and limiting these to the two notions truth and formula might seem highly desirable. Truth is a notion that some nominalists think they are entitled to anyway; and if formulas (in the sense of formula types, whether exemplified by any actual inscriptions or not) are "abstract entities", and hence non-nominalistic, still they are relatively clear ones.

In the case of pure mathematics, the answer seems to be that a certain part of mathematics can be developed using only predicative set theory, provided we allow predicative sets of objects other than physical objects. E.g., if we consider the formulas of N to be themselves individuals of some other language M, and then build up a series of languages M, M', M'', . . . as sketched before, we can develop at least the arithmetic of rational numbers, and a rudimentary theory of functions by rational numbers. (We need some infinite domain of individuals to "get started", however, which is why we have to take nonconcrete objects, e.g., formulas as individuals, unless we are willing to postulate the existence of an actual infinity of physical objects.) Unfortunately, no satisfactory theory of real numbers or of real functions can be obtained in this way, which is why most mathematicians reject the predicative standpoint.

Turning to logic, i.e.. to the notion of "validity", we say early in this essay that a notion of validity, namely "truth of all substitution-instances" (in, say, M), could be defined in what are essentially the terms of predicative set theory (truth, and quantification over formulas). We also saw that a more satisfactory notion requires the use of the expression "all sets"—i.e., the notions of impredicative set theory.

Turning lastly to physics, we find the following. At first blush, the law of gravitation (we shall pretend this is the only law of physics, in the present essay) requires quantification over *real* numbers.

However, the law is equivalent to the statement that for every rational ε, and all rational m_1, m_2, d, there is a rational δ such that

$$\text{if } M_a = m_1 \pm \delta, M_b = m_2 \pm \delta, d = d_1 \pm \delta,$$

then

$$F = \frac{g m_1 m_2}{d_1} \pm \varepsilon$$

and this statement quantifies only over rational numbers. (There is the problem that the gravitational constant g may not be rational, however! which I shall neglect here.) Thus a language which quantifies only over *rational* numbers and which measures distances, masses, forces, etc., only by rational approximations ("the mass of a is $m_1 \pm \delta$") *is*, in principle, strong enough to at least *state* the law of gravitation.

Given just predicative set theory, one can easily define the rational numbers. Also one has enough set theory to define "the cardinal number of S", where S is any *definable* finite set of physical things. Handling the "numericalization" of such physical magnitudes as distance, force, mass using rational approximations and predicative sets is quite complicated, but still perfectly possible. Thus it appears *possible* (though complicated and awkward) to do physics using just predicative set theory.

In summary, then, the set theoretic "needs" of physics are surprisingly similar to the set theoretic needs of pure logic. Both disciplines need *some* set

theory to function at all. Both disciplines can "live"
—but live badly—on the meager diet of only predicative sets. Both can live extremely happily on the rich
diet of impredicative sets. Insofar, then, as the indispensability of quantification over sets is any argument for their existence—and we will discuss why it
is in the next section—we may say that it is a strong
argument for the existence of at least predicative
sets, and a pretty strong, but not *as* strong, argument
for the existence of impredicative sets. When we
come to the higher reaches of set theory, however—
sets of sets of sets of sets—we come to conceptions
which are today not needed outside of pure mathematics itself. The case for "realism" being developed in the present chapter is thus a qualified one: at
least sets of things, real numbers, and functions from
various kinds of things to real numbers should be accepted as part of the presently indispensable (or
nearly indispensable) framework of both physical
science and logic, and as part of that whose existence
we are presently committed to. But sets of very high
type or very high cardinality (higher than the con-
tinuum, for example), should today be investigated
in an "if-then" spirit. One day they may be as indispensable to the very *statement* of physical laws
as, say, rational numbers are today; then doubt of
their "existence" will be as futile as extreme nominalism now is. But for the present we should regard
them as what they are—speculative and daring extensions of the basic mathematical apparatus of
science.

VIII.
Indispensability Arguments

So far I have been developing an argument for
realism along roughly the following lines: quantification over mathematical entities is indispensable
for science, both formal and physical; therefore we
should accept such quantification; but this commits
us to accepting the existence of the mathematical
entities in question. This type of argument stems, of
course, from Quine, who has for years stressed both
the indispensability of quantification over mathematical entities and the intellectual dishonesty of
denying the existence of what one daily presupposes.
But indispensability arguments raise a number of
questions, some of which I should like briefly to discuss here.

One question which may be raised, for example,
concerns the very intelligibility of such sentences as
"numbers exist", "sets exist", "functions from
space-time points to real numbers exist", etc. If
these are not genuine assertions at all but only, so to
speak, pseudo-assertions, then *no* argument can be
a good argument for believing them, and *a fortiori*

"indispensability arguments" cannot be good arguments for believing them.

But what reason is there to say that "numbers exist", "sets exist", etc., are unintelligible? It may be suggested that *something* must be wrong with these "assertions", since one comes across them only in *philosophy*. But there is something extremely dubious about this mode of argument, currently fashionable though it may be. It is one thing to *show* that the locutions upon which a particular philosophical problem depends are linguistically deviant. If, indeed, *no* way can be found of stating the alleged "problem" which does *not* involve doing violence to the language, then the suspicion may be justified that the "problem" is no clear problem at all; though, even so, it would hardly amount to certainty, since linguistically deviant expressions need not always be literally *unintelligible*. But it is no argument at all against the genuineness of a putative philosophical problem or assertion that its key terms are linguistically deviant (or, more informally, "odd", or "queer", or whatever), if that "deviancy" (or "oddness", or "queerness", or whatever) was only established in the first place by appealing to the dubious principle that terms and statements that occur only in philosophy are *ipso facto* deviant. For the difficulty (it appears to be more than "difficulty", in fact) is that there is no *linguistic* evidence for this startling claim. Every discipline has terms and statements peculiar to it; and there is no reason whatsoever why the same should not be true of philosophy. If the statement

"material objects exist", for example, does not
occur outside of philosophy, that is because only
philosophers are concerned with what entitles us to
believe such an obvious proposition, and only philosophers have the patience and professional training
to pursue a question of justification that turns out to
be so difficult; what other science is concerned with
entitlement and justification as such? Although the
claim is frequently heard that philosophical propositions are by their very nature linguistically (or logically, or "conceptually") confused, not one shred of
linguistic evidence exists to show that such sentences
as "numbers exist", "sets exist", and "material
objects exist", for that matter, are *linguistically*
deviant; i.e., that these sentences violate any norms
of natural language that can be ascertained to *be*
norms of natural language by appropriate scientific
procedures.

To put it another way; it would be startling and
important if we could honestly *show* that locutions
which are peculiar to philosophical discourse have
something linguistically wrong with them; but it is
uninteresting to claim that this is so if the "evidence"
for the claim is merely that certain particular locutions which are peculiar to philosophy *must* have
something wrong with them *because* they are peculiar
to philosophy and *because locutions which occur
only in philosophical discourse are "odd."* The form
of the argument is a straightforward circle: a principle *P* (that there is something wrong with locutions
which occur only in philosophical discourse) is ad-

vanced; many supporting examples are given for the principle *P* (i.e., of philosophical statements and questions which are allegedly "odd", "queer", etc.); but it turns out that these supporting examples *are* supporting examples only if the principle *P* is assumed. I do not deny that, historically, many philosophical statements and arguments have contained (and, in some cases, essentially depended upon) locutions which are "queer" by any standard. What I claim is that there is nothing linguistically "queer" about general existence questions ("do numbers exist?", "do material objects exist?") *per se,* nor about general questions of justification or entitlement ("what entitles us to believe that material objects exist?"), either. (Yet these latter questions are rejected, and by just the circular reasoning just described, in John L. Austin's book *Sense and Sensibilia,* for example; and I am sure many philosophers would similarly reject the former questions.)

So far I have argued that there is no reason to classify such assertions as "numbers exist" and "sets exist" as linguistically deviant, apart from a philosophical principle which appears completely misguided. Moreover, there is an easy way to bypass this question completely. Even if some philosophers would reject the sentence "numbers exist" as somehow not in the normal language, still, "numbers exist with the property——" is admitted to be non-deviant (and even true) for many values of "——". For example, "numbers exist with the property of being prime and greater than 10^{10}", is certainly non-deviant and true. Then, if it should indeed be the case that "numbers exist" *simpliciter* is not in the language, we could always bring it into the language by simply introducing it as a new speech-form, with the accompanying stipulation that "numbers exist" is to be true if and only if there is a condition "——" such that "numbers exist with the property ——" is true.

What this amounts to is this: if the sentence

(1) $(\exists x) (x$ is a number $\cdot x$ is prime $\cdot x > 10^{10})$

(i.e., the sentence so symbolized) is in the language, while

(2) $(\exists x) (x$ is a number$)$

(i.e., "numbers exist") is not in the language, then ordinary language is not "deductively closed": for (2) is deducible from (1) in standard logic (by the theorem "$(\exists x) (Fx \cdot Gx \cdot Hx) \supset (\exists x)Fx$"). But if ordinary language is not deductively closed in this respect, then we can deductively close it by introducing (2) into the language, and, moreover, this can be done in essentially just one way. So we may as well count (2) as part of the language to begin with.

We have now rejected the view that "numbers exist", "sets exist", etc., are linguistically deviant, do not possess a truth-value, etc.

A second reason that certain philosophers might advance for rejecting indispensability arguments is the following: these philosophers claim that the truths of logic and mathematics are *true by conven-*

tion. If, in particular, "numbers exist" and "sets exist" are true by convention, then considerations of dispensability or indispensability are *irrelevant.*

This "conventionalist" position founders, however, as soon as the conventonalist is asked to become specific about details. *Exactly how* is the notion of truth, as applied to sentences which quantify over abstract entities, to be defined in terms of the notion of *convention?* Even assuming that *some* mathematical sentences *are* "true by convention", in the sense of being *immediately* true by convention, and that these could be listed, the conventionalist still requires some notion of *implication* in order to handle those truths of mathematics which are not, on any view, immediately conventional—i.e., which require proof. But the notion of implication (validity of the conditional) is one which requires set theory to define, as we have seen; thus conventionalism, even if correct, presupposes quantification over abstract entities, as something intelligible apart from the notion of a convention; mathematical truth ends up being explained as truth by virtue of immediate convention *and mathematics*—an explanation which is trivially correct (apart from the important question of just how large the conventional element in mathematics really is). Moreover, if the conventionalist is not careful, his theory of mathematical truth may easily end up by being in conflict with results of mathematics itself—in particular, with Gödel's theorem. However, discussion of this topic would lead us too far afield; for now I shall simply dismiss conventionalism on the ground that no one has been able to *state* the alleged view in a form which is at all precise and which does not immediately collapse.

A third reason that philosophers might once have given for rejecting indispensability arguments is the following: around the turn of the century a number of philosophers claimed that various entities presupposed by scientific and common sense discourse—even, in the case of some of these philosophers, material objects themselves—were merely "useful fictions", or that we can not, at any rate, possibly know that they are *more* than "useful fictions" (and so we may as well say that that is what they are). This "fictionalistic" philosophy seems presently to have disappeared; but it is necessary to consider it here for a moment, if only because it represents the most direct possible rejection of the probative force of indispensability arguments. For the fictionalist says, in substance *"Yes,* certain concepts—material object, number, set, etc.—are indispensable, but *no,* that has no tendency to show that entities corresponding to those concepts actually exist. It only shows that those 'entities' are *useful fictions."*

If fictionalism has been rejected by present-day philosophers of science and epistemologists, this appears to have been in part for bad reasons. The fictionalists regarded the following as a logical possibility: that there might not in fact be electrons (or whatever), but that our experiences might be *as if* there were actually electrons (or whatever). According to the verificationism popular since the late 1920s, this is *meaningless*: if p is a proposition which it would be logically impossible to verify, then p does not represent so much as a logical possibility. But on this issue the fictionalists were surely right and the verificationists wrong: it may be absurd, or crazy, or silly, or totally irrational to believe that, e.g., we are all disembodied spirits under the thought control of some powerful intelligence whose chief purpose is to deceive us into thinking that there is a material world; but it is not *logically impossible*. This is not an essay on verificationism; but it is appropriate to say in passing that all of the verificationist arguments were bad arguments. The chief argument was, of course, to contend that "material objects exist" *means* something to the effect that under certain circumstances we tend to have certain experiences; but all attempts to carry out the program of actually supplying a reduction of material object language to "sense-datum" language have failed utterly, and today it seems almost certainly the case that no such reduction can be carried out. Given a large body of theory T, containing both "sense-datum" sentences and "thing sentences" (assuming, for the sake of charity, that a "sense datum" language could really be constructed), one could say what "sense datum" sentences are logically implied by T, to be sure; but this does not mean that the thing-sentences in T (much less in "the language" considered apart from any particular theory) must be individually equivalent to sense-datum sentences in any reasonable sense of "equivalent". Another argument was a species of open-question argument: "What more does it mean to say that material objects exist, than that under such-and-such conditions we tend to have such-and-such experiences?" But the open-question argument presupposes the success of phenomenalistic reduction. If you have a translation S' of a thing sentence S into phenomenalistic language, then it is well and good to ask "what more does S mean than S'?", but you must not ask this rhetorical question unless you have constructed S'. Another play was to say: "Pseudo-hypotheses, like the one about the demon, have only *picture meaning*". Besides representing an objectionable form of argument (namely, assuming the philosophical point at issue and explaining your opponent's propensity to error psychologically), this contention is just false. The "demon hypothesis" is not just a *noise* that happens to evoke some "pictures in the head"; it is a grammatical sentence in a language; it is one we can offer free translations of; it is subject to linguistic transformations; we can deduce other statements from it and also say what other statements imply it; we can say whether it is linguistically appropriate or inappropriate in a given context, and whether a discourse containing it is linguistically regular or deviant. The verificationists would retort: "It doesn't follow it has *meaning*". But they would just be wrong, for this is just what meaning is: being meaningful is being subject to certain kinds of recursive transformations, and to certain kinds of regularities; we may not know much more about the matter than that today, but we know enough to know that what the verificationists were propounding was not an analysis of meaning but a persuasive redefinition. The worst argument of all, however, was the one which ran as follows: "If you *do* admit the demon hypothesis as a logical possibility, then you will be doomed to utter scepticism; for you will never be able to offer any reason to say that it is false." In case anyone needs to hear a reply to this claim, that verificationism and verificationism alone can save us all from the bogey of scepticism here is one: If the demon hypothesis is so constructed as to lead to exactly the same testable consequences as the more plausible system of hypotheses that we actually believe (or to the same testable consequences as any system of hypotheses that rational men would find more plausible), then it is not logically false, but it is logically impossible that it should ever be rational to believe it. For rationality requires that when two hypotheses H_1, H_2 lead to the same testable predictions (either at all times, or at the present), and H_1 is *a priori* much more plausible than H_2, then H_1 should be given the preference over H_2. If, in particular, H_1 has been accepted, and all hypotheses *a priori* more plausible than H_1 have led to a false prediction, then we should not give up H_1 merely because someone confronts us with a *logical possibility* of its being false. (This is roughly Newton's "rule 4" in *Principia*.)

But, it may be asked, "is there really such a thing

as *a priori* plausibility?'' The answer is that it is
easily shown that all possible inductive logics depend
implicitly or explicitly on this: An *a priori* ordering
of hypotheses on the basis of ''simplicity'', or on the
basis of the kinds of predicates they contain, or of
the form of the laws they propose, or some other
basis. To refuse to make any *a priori decisions* as to
which hypotheses are more or less plausible is just
to commit oneself to never making any inductive ex-
trapolation from past experience at all; for at any
given time infinitely many mutually incompatible
hypotheses are each compatible with any finite
amount of data, so that if we ever declare that a
hypothesis has been ''confirmed'', it is not because
all other hypotheses have been ruled out, but because all the remaining hypotheses are rejected as
too implausible even though they agree with and even
predict the evidence—i.e., at some point hypotheses
must be rejected on *a priori* grounds if any hypothesis is ever to be accepted at all. Again, the sceptic
will object, ''How do you know the demon hypothesis
is less plausible than the normal hypothesis?'' But
the answer is that to accept a plausibility ordering is
neither to make a judgment of empirical fact nor to
state a theorem of deductive logic; it is to take a
methodological stand. One can only say whether the
demon hypothesis is ''crazy'' or not if one has taken
such a stand; I report the stand I have taken (and,
speaking as one who has taken this stand, I add: and
the stand all rational men take, implicitly or explicitly). In sum, we can ''rule out'' the demon hypoth-

esis without playing fast and loose with the notion of
logical impossibility or with the notion of mean-
inglessness; we have only to admit that we have
taken a stand according to which this hypothesis is
a priori less probable than the normal hypothesis,
and then observe the peculiar fact: it is a logical
truth (because of the way the demon hypothesis
was constructed) that if the demon (hypothesis) is
true, it cannot be rational to believe it (assuming,
of course, the following maxim of rationality: Do
not believe H_1 if all the phenomena accounted for by
H_1 are accounted for also by H_2, and H_2 is more
plausible than H_1). But if it is a logical truth (relative to the above maxim of rationality) that it would
always be irrational to believe the demon hypothesis,
then that is enough; if we can justify rejecting it, we
need not feel compelled to go further and try to show
that it does not represent even a logical possibility.

Another fashionable way of rejecting fictionalism
has its roots in instrumentalism rather than in verificationism. One encounters, for example, somewhat
the following line of reasoning: to ask whether statements are "true" cannot be separated from asking
whether it is rational to accept those statements (so
far, so good), since it is rational to accept *p is true*
just in case it is rational to accept *p*. But the end purpose of our whole "conceptual system" is just the
prediction and control of experience (or that plus
"simplicity", whatever that is). The fictionalist concedes that the conceptual system of material objects
(or whatever) leads to successful prediction (or as

successful as we have been able to manage to date) and that it is as simple as we have been able to manage to date. But these are just the factors on which rational acceptance depends; so it is rational to accept our conceptual system, and rational to call the propositions that make it up "true" (or "as true as anything is", in Anthony Quinton's happy phrase, since we always reserve the right to change our minds).

Now, there is unquestionably some insight in this retort to fictionalism. Elementary as the point may be, it is correct to remind the fictionalist that we cannot separate the grounds which make it rational to accept a proposition p from the grounds which make it rational to accept p *is true*. I myself dislike talk of simplicity, because simplicity in any measurable sense (e.g., length of the expressions involved, or number of logical connectives, or number of argument places of the predicates involved) is only *one* of the factors affecting the judgments of relative plausibility that scientists and rational men actually make, and by no means the most important one. But this is not a crucial point; we have only to recognize that the instrumentalist is using the word simplicity to stand for a complicated matter depending on many factors, notwithstanding some misleading connotations the word may have. The fictionalist concedes that predicative power and "simplicity" (i.e., overall plausibility in comparison with rival hypotheses, as scientists and rational men actually judge these matters) are the hallmarks of a good theory, and that they make it rational to accept a theory, at least "for scientific purposes". But then—and it is the good feature of the instrumentalist strategy to press this devastating question home to the fictionalist—what *further* reasons could one want before one regarded it as rational to *believe* a theory? If the very things that make the fictionalist regard material objects, etc., as "useful fictions" do not make it rational to believe the material object "conceptual system", what could make it rational to believe anything?

Historically, fictionalists split into two camps in the face of this sort of question. A theological fictionalist like Duhem maintained that Thomistic metaphysics (and metaphysics alone) could establish propositions about reality as true; science could only show that certain propositions are useful for prediction and systematization of data. A sceptical fictionalist like Hans Vaihinger maintained, on the other hand, that nothing could establish that, e.g., material objects really exist; we can only know that they are useful fictions. But neither move is satisfactory. Inquirers not precommitted to the Catholic Church do not agree that Thomistic metaphysics is a superior road to truth than modern science; and scepticism only reduces to a futile and silly demand that a deductive (or some kind of *a priori*) justification be given for the basic standards of inductive inquiry, or else that they be abandoned. Moreover, there is something especially pathetic about the sceptical version of fictionalism; for Vaihinger and his followers in the philosophy of "As-If" did not doubt that science will lead to (approximately) correct prediction, and thereby they did accept induction at one point (notwithstanding the lack of a deductive justification), although they refused to believe that science leads to *true* theories, and thereby rejected induction (or the hypothetico-deductive method, which Mill correctly regarded as the most powerful method of the inductive sciences) at another point. Why can we never know that scientific theories are true? Because, the fictionalist said, we can give no deductive proof that they are true, even assuming all possible observational knowledge. But neither can we give a deductive proof that the sun will rise tomorrow! The fictionalist was thus a halfhearted skeptic; he chose to accept induction partially (as leading to successful prediction of experience), but not totally (as leading to true belief about things).

While I agree so far with the instrumentalist strategy of argument, I am deeply disturbed by one point; the premise that the purpose of science is prediction of experience (or that plus "simplicity", where simplicity is some kind of a funny aim-in-itself and not a rubric for a large number of factors affecting our judgment of probable truth). This premise makes it easy to refute the fictionalist: for if there is no difference between believing p and believing that p leads to successful prediction (at least when p is a whole conceptual system), then fictionalism immediately collapses. But this is just verificationism again, except that now "the unit of meaning is the whole conceptual system''. It is hard to believe that there is such a thing as "the aim of science"— there are many aims of many scientists; and it is just not the case that all scientists are primarily interested in prediction. Some scientists are primarily interested in, for example, discovering certain facts about radio stars, or genes, or mesons, or what have you. They want successful predictions in order to confirm their theories; they do not want theories in order to obtain the predictions, which are in some cases of not the slightest interest in themselves, but of interest only because they tend to establish the truth or falsity of some theory. Also, it is just not the case that simplicity is a thing that all scientists value as an end in itself; many scientists only care about simplicity because and when it is evidence of truth. At bottom the only relevant difference between the following two statements:

(3)   The aim of science is successful prediction

and

(4)   An aim of some scientists is to know whether or not it is true that mesons behave in such-and-such a way

besides the incredible pomposity of (3) ("the aim of science" indeed!), is that (3) is couched in observation language. But why should the aim of science, if there is such a thing, or even the aims of all scientists, be statable in observation language any more than the content of science is expressible in observation language? Surely this is just a hangover from reductionism!

In sum, fictionalism has on the whole been rejected for a bad reason: because verificationism has made the perfectly sound and elementary distinction between truth of scientific theory and truth of its observational consequences unpopular, and thereby dismissed just the point—the apparent gap between the two—that worried the fictionalists. But, as we have also seen, there is a rejoinder to fictionalism that does not depend on reductionist views about either the content or the "aim" of science. The rejoinder is simply that the very factors that make it rational to accept a theory "for scientific purposes" also make it rational to believe it, at least in the sense in which one ever "believes" a scientific theory—as an approximation to the truth which can probably be bettered, and not as a final truth. Fictionalism fails because (Duhem to the contrary) it could not exhibit a better method for fixing our belief than the scientific method, and because (Vaihinger to the contrary) the absence of a deductive justification for the scientific method in no way shows that it is not rational to accept it.

At this point we have considered the rejoinder to indispensability arguments, viz., that it might be indispensable to believe p but that p might nonetheless really be false, and we have rejected ths rejoinder, not for the usual verificationist or instrumentalist reasons, which seem to rest on false doctrines, but because it is silly to agree that a reason for believing that p warrants accepting p in all scientific circumstances, and then to add—"but even so it is not *good enough*". Such a judgment could only be made if one accepted a transscientific method as superior to the scientific method; but this philosopher, at least, has no interest in doing *that*.

IX.

Unconsidered Complications

———◆•◆•◆———

In this essay, I have chosen to go into detail on one group of questions—those having to do with the indispensability of quantification over abstract entities such as sets—at the cost of having to neglect many others. One group of questions which I might have considered has to do with the existence of what I might call "equivalent constructions" in mathematics. For example, numbers can be constructed from *sets* in more than one way. Moreover, the notion of *set* is not the *only* notion which can be taken as basic; we have already indicated that predicative set theory, at least, is in some sense intertranslatable with talk of formulas and truth; and even the impredicative notion of set admits of various equivalents: for example, instead of identifying functions with certain *sets,* as I did, I might have identified *sets* with certain functions. My own view is that none of these approaches should be regarded as "more true" than any other; the realm of mathematical fact admits of many "equivalent descriptions": but clearly a whole essay could have been devoted to *this*.

Again, we discussed very briefly the interesting topic of conventionalism. Even if the conventionalist view has never been made very plausible (or even clear), it raises fascinating issues. The question of to what extent we might revise our basic logical principles, as we have had to revise some of our basic geometrical principles in mathematical physics, is an especially fascinating one. Today, the tendency among philosophers is to assume that in no sense does logic itself have an empirical foundation. I believe that this tendency is wrong; but this issue too has had to be avoided rather than discussed in the present chapter. My purpose has been to give some idea of the many-layered complexity which one encounters in attacking even one part of the philosophy of logic; but I hope I have not left the impression that the part discussed in this book is all there is.